SCHOLASTIC
News
Nonfiction Readers

Newts and Other Amphibians

by
Mary Schulte

Children's Press®
A Division of Scholastic Inc.
New York Toronto London Auckland Sydney
Mexico City New Delhi Hong Kong
Danbury, Connecticut

These content vocabulary word builders
are for grades 1-2.

Consultant:
C. Kenneth Dodd, Jr., Ph.D.

Curriculum Specialist: Linda Bullock

Special thanks to Omaha's Henry Doorly Zoo

Photo Credits:

Photographs © 2005: Animals Animals/Steven David Miller: 23 top left; Corbis Images: 23 bottom right (Amos Nachoum), 17, 21 bottom (Chris Taylor/Cordaiy Photo Library Ltd.); Dan Suzio Photography: 4 bottom right, 11, 21 top, 23 bottom left; Dembinsky Photo Assoc./Skip Moody: cover right inset; Minden Pictures: cover center inset, 5 top right, 19 (Michael & Patricia Fogden), cover background, 1, 2, 4 bottom left, 12, 13 (Rene Krekels/Foto Natura); Nature Picture Library Ltd.: 5 bottom left, 7, 20 top (Jeff Foott), back cover (David Welling); Photo Researchers, NY: 23 top right (E. R. Degginger), cover left inset, 4 top, 15 (Dante Fenolio), 5 top left, 5 bottom right, 9, 20 bottom (Dave Roberts/SPL).

Book Design: Simonsays Design!

Library of Congress Cataloging-in-Publication Data

Schulte, Mary, 1958-
   Newts and other amphibians / by Mary Schulte.
      p. cm. – (Scholastic news nonfiction readers)
   Includes bibliographical references and index.
   ISBN 0-516-24934-7 (lib. bdg.)
   1. Amphibians–Juvenile literature. I. Title. II. Series.
   QL644.2.S339 2005
   597.8–dc22

                                           2005003295

1 2 3 4 5 6 7 8 9 10 R 14 13 12 11 10 09 08 07 06 05

CONTENTS

WORD HUNT

Look for these words as you read. They will be in **bold**.

amphibian
(am-**fib**-ee-uhn)

gills
(gils)

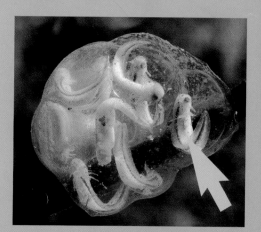

larva
(**lar**-vuh)

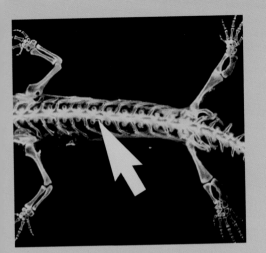

backbone
(**bak**-bone)

caecilian
(suh-**sil**-yuhn)

newt
(noot)

vertebrate
(**vur**-tuh-brate)

5

Amphibians!

What is an **amphibian**?

An amphibian is an animal with moist skin.

Most amphibians do not have scales.

Toads, frogs, and salamanders are amphibians.
So are **newts**.

This newt's skin looks
wet. It is very moist.

Amphibians are **vertebrates**.

Vertebrates are animals with **backbones**.

Newts have backbones.

That means newts are vertebrates.

backbone

Look at this X-ray photo of a newt!

Most amphibians come from eggs.

Newts lay their eggs in water. The eggs hatch.

Baby newts are called **larvae.**

These larvae will hatch soon.

The newt larvae live in the water. They use their **gills** to breathe.

Soon the larvae will change.

They will start to use their lungs to breathe.

gill

This newt has gills on the side of its head. They look like feathers.

Amphibians can breathe through their skin, too!

Salamanders are amphibians.

Some salamanders don't have lungs.

They breathe through their skin instead.

This is a salamander that does have lungs.

Amphibians are cold-blooded.

The temperature inside an amphibian changes to match the temperature outside.

Toads are amphibians.

When the air is warm, toads are warm.

When the air is cold, toads are cold.

This is not an earthworm.

It is a **Caecilian**.

Worms do not have backbones, but these animals do.

Caecilians even have teeth.

Caecilians are amphibians!

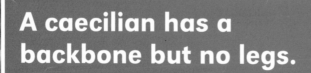
A caecilian has a backbone but no legs.

WHAT IS AN AMPHIBIAN?

Amphibians have moist skin. Their skin looks wet.

Amphibians have backbones.

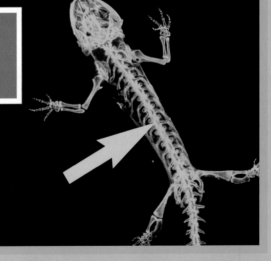

Most amphibians come from eggs.

Amphibians are cold-blooded.

YOUR NEW WORDS

amphibian (am-**fib**-ee-uhn) an animal with a backbone and moist skin

backbone (**bak**-bone) the bones that run down the middle of the back

caecilian (suh-**sil**-yuhn) an amphibian with no arms and no legs that looks like a large worm

gills (gils) the body part that larvae use to breathe under the water

larva (**lar**-vuh) the early form of an animal that hatches in the water

newt (noot) a small amphibian with short legs and a long tail that lives on land

vertebrate (**vur**-tuh-brate) an animal with a backbone

IS IT AN AMPHIBIAN?

Alligator
(No. It's a reptile.)

Earthworm
(No. It's an annelid.)

Lizard
(No. It's a reptile.)

Stingray
(No. It's a fish.)

23

INDEX

FIND OUT MORE
Book:
Newts, by Lola M. Schaefer (Reed Educational & Professional Publishing, 2002)

Website:
http://nationalzoo.si.edu/Animals/ReptilesAmphibians/default.cfm

MEET THE AUTHOR:

Mary Schulte is a newspaper photo editor and author of books and articles for children. She is the author of the other animal classification books in this series. She lives in Kansas City, Missouri, where she has never run into a newt.